Destination: unknown

A Poetic Journey

Second Edition

by,

Brianni Davis

Copyright © 2011 Brianni Davis

All rights reserved.

DEDICATION

to those who have weathered my storms:

I am eternally grateful for you

so, to you, I write

...for Aubrielle Nikai and James Blue:

every breath I take is for the two of you

CONTENTS

Admiration	1
Amazing	3
Angry	9
Appreciation	12
Change	16
Fill in the Blank	20
Get It Together	23
Her Worth	26
Kiss It	31
Little Big Girl	36
Me to You	38
Thirsty	42
Not The One	45
Single Mother Speaks	48
Text Message	52
The Cycle	56
B List Rapper	61
RIP	63
Pretender	66
Shit	69
Beautifully Black	73
Can I Be	78
That Man	83
Calling You Out	88
False Realities	92
Break Up No Make Up	96
Always Crying	101
Deep	105
My People	110
My Poem Speaks	117
Promiscuity	123
Sometimes I Wonder	128
Truth	134
Glamour	142
Just Me	147
Price Tags	154

Admiration

If I had wings
I would choose to give them to you
because I want you to soar
you define achievement
should be recognized/acknowledged/commended
for what the coming days have in store for you
life is not easy
as a Black man you are
challenged daily/berated mentally
told to hold back emotionally and show no signs of weakness
oh how I wish I could be your strength
hold you up with invisible hands
whenever you find yourself faltering
pull you along with fingers dipped in admiration
whenever you're falling behind
and sometimes
I just want to stand
in a corner
and watch you shine
because you define perseverance
perfectly imperfect in so many ways
you are a King even without a throne
prone to mistakes like the average man
yet average is an insult to the likes of you
you are a splendid Black man
unselfishly gave me the privilege to walk beneath the glow

of the aura that hovers over you

in a past life I think I was you

and if not

in a future one I'd like to be you

carved out of butterscotch-maple-chocolate

caramel-toffee-coffee-colored

masculinity

features chiseled with tools of greatness

hands big and strong and wide enough

to encompass your world

heart outlined in red, black and green

you bleed dignity/sweat diligence/breathe integrity

and I'm watching you become the very best there is

watching you morph into what they said you would never be

watching you overcome obstacles

and side-step roadblocks

and laugh in the face of adversity

I adore you

admire you

respect you

and wish I could protect you from harms that may befall you

instead I will stand nearby in silence

hoping my constant presence

is enough to show you I appreciate you

for who you were

who you are

and who I am confident you will become

Amazing

If nobody told you you're beautiful today
then let me be the first
I know you looked in the mirror this morning
and realized your reflection wasn't smiling back at you
maybe you thought your hair wasn't straight or long enough
your skin wasn't clear or light enough
your nose wasn't thin or pointy enough
but if I was standing there beside you
I would have told you that you
are amazing
as women we are taught to be wary of those who share our gender
bred to be cautious of women who try to befriend us
for fear that they have ulterior motives
our jealousy of others is apparent yet we still try to hide it
instead of complimenting her on her style and dress
we find ourselves searching intently for her flaws
voicing our displeasure for all to see
hoping, wishing, silently
that in some ways, we were she
because we're never really content with being we
being us
or I guess I should say being me
because I never thought I was good enough
bought into the hype that I could find
pretty in a bottle
sexy in a dress

thick in a plate of soul food
toned in a gym
always looking for a quick remedy to be more appealing to him
to them
to those who found ways to degrade
without ever really trying
yet, I exuded confidence with every step
had mouthpiece that couldn't be met
and game that consistently let me stay on top
would spend hours in a club
with a cute ass outfit on sucking my stomach in
never sitting down because doing so
would make the balls of my feet burn
from the stilettos I'd worn hoping to stand out
if I wasn't the center of attention
then I was normal
average at best
too close for comfort to fitting in with the rest
so I pretended
said I would fake it til I make it and walked around smiling
grinning from ear to ear while refusing to hear my inner voice
the one telling me to slow down, take a step back and retract
because I was living life in the fast lane
thinking that casual encounters would allow me to gain
notoriety
hell, it worked for him…and him…and him
so why not me

why was I so wrong to chase and replace
to sleep with her man and then smile in her face
to get high with them and drink until my heart was content
but then hold up that degree
I got in 3 years from Berkeley
as though that meant I'd somehow made it
when in reality, I was just starting out
trying to find myself when I didn't know I was lost
heal myself when I didn't realize I was ill
fix myself when I didn't know I was broken
because someone looked me in my eyes
and told me I was amazing
said I was beautiful as though it were a matter of fact
rather than opinion
but that it didn't matter what he thought
if I didn't believe it myself
and that opened my eyes
made me realize the demise of my greatness
would come sooner than I wanted it to
if I didn't step it up
see, potential is nothing more than a word
with no actions to back it up so I took heed
told myself I had to take the lead
in the story that is my life
which brings me to the here and now, to you
and I'm telling you that you are beautiful
no matter what negative things may have been said to you

you are amazing
capable of creating changes unimaginable to most
you are brilliant
placed in positions to find ways to make the world a better place
it doesn't matter what
he said/she said/they said
or somehow led you to believe
I'm asking you to believe me
you are God's greatest creation
they say man needed an even stronger being to stand by his side
and that's you-
don't you recognize your greatness?
you have the ability to give life
passing on your strengths, triumphs and pride
so stop selling yourself so short
from one woman to another, I admire you
the courage it takes to get up and face a society
who hardly used to see you as a human being is commendable
and you deserve recognition, appreciation and honor
so as a young Black woman in training
I challenge you to be you
stand out when it's unpopular to do so
reach out and allow yourself to be helped by others
speak out against those who have put you down
do your very best to excel in all that you do
because you're a WOMAN
and we are born and bred to be ready, willing, and determined

strong, steadfast, and forthcoming
so demand respect
command attention
act as you speak and think
and believe me when I tell you as I was told
that you are amazing
whether you're sliding down a pole
working a stage
or doing something strange for a lil' piece of change
if you have an AA, a BA or no A
if you're a struggling single mother
or unattached and on your own
if you have the support of your family
or are a lost soul in a pack of many
we share a common bond
now if you hear me, then do this:
stand up
with one toe, draw a line in front of both your feet
that line represents those who've doubted you
now take one step forward
look down
guess what?
you've just crossed the line of defeat!
keep standing
take a look to your right and your left-
we are a force to be reckoned with
and if someone tells you differently

just say
"well, Brianni thinks I'M the SHIT!"
you are amazing...

Angry

I don't apologize for my anger
won't write nice sweet poetry
for the men who can't handle when I get a little too "real"
so stop coming up to me when I step off the mic
and asking me not to be so angry
I will stop being angry when I stop seeing 13 year olds
pushing strollers in between junior high school classes
when I stop hearing "stuck up bitch"
come out of the mouth of a man who got denied a phone number
when I stop watching single mothers
half-heartedly search for their third job
because ends still never quite seem to meet
when they are the only ones financially responsible
for the kids it took two to create
I'll stop being angry when my people stop selling narcotics
within 15 feet of elementary schools
when my male counterparts stop thinking
a couple shots of patron they're willing to buy me at the bar
would be enough to part my thighs
with or without my consent
I'll stop being angry when people start being honest about their intentions
when people realize I'm not a bitter woman
some of you just leave a bitter taste in my mouth
every time I'm in your presence
see you say I never talk about the 'Good Black Men'

but that's bullshit
because I give praise to those who deserve it
your ears just perk up when I speak on that "nigga shit"
so maybe some of this applies to you
more than you originally thought it did
yes I'm angry
I'm angry at the fact that women think they have to
degrade themselves on reality shows
to compete for the attention of one man
because so many others have failed to build their hope
in ordinary men being attracted to them
I'm angry because too many men are quick to fuck a woman in private
but call her a hoe when they're in the company of their friends
I'm angry because too many are content with being
baby daddies and baby mamas
yet complain when their kids run wild
as though being the products of shattered households
have not contributed to that behavior
I'm angry because my 25 yr old brother
who will remain behind bars for the next 40 years to life
thinks I should hook him up with one of my friends
as though he has something to offer them
I'm angry because people put poets who express themselves on this mic
up on a pedestal we never asked to be placed on
then get mad and call us hypocrites

when we fall off and you see we're just human
I'm angry
and fuck you if you have a problem with that
fuck you if you're upset that I didn't write a poem about you
when I saw you at the park with your daughter
wearing matching Daddy & Me shirts
because I'm not going to make a big ass deal
about you doing what you're supposed to in the first place
fuck you if you can detect my anger from a mile away
at those who thought a girl from Richmond CA being gang raped and videotaped
didn't deserve national attention
because I'm sure it happens more often than young women will ever mention
fuck you for telling me not to be angry
maybe the real problem is too many of us aren't angry enough
too many of us are too complacent
too comfortable with accepting bullshit served on a platter
as though that changes its form
as though it's the norm
to settle
so yes I'm angry
and I have every reason to be
and from now on you will no longer receive
apologies from me
for my angry ass honesty

Appreciation

It's easy to complain about

the men who have done us wrong

the "niggas" who took advantage

the losers who broke our hearts

but it's not so easy to admit the role we, as women

play in these situations

so it's time I own up

if I'm a spokesperson for women when we feel we're right

I have to be the scapegoat for us when I know we're wrong

we have scandalous tendencies

sometimes acting like we really like you

when really, we only want sex from you but don't want to be

labeled a hoe

we chant the words to all the

"Independent Women" songs we hear

but get upset when you don't open doors, pay for dates or

walk on the outside of us

we want you to have 6 figure salaries

even though we're still taking out student loans

we tell you all our girls' sexual business

but are quick to want to leave you when you experience it firsthand

as though we didn't plant the seed of curiosity

we cheat

not all of us

but enough of us for me to admit it with a straight face

we think flirting is harmless but will cuss you out

if your eyes linger on her butt just a little too long for our comfort
sometimes… we lie
no, the text message we received while we were laying next to you
in bed
was not our sister, best friend or "play brother"
we just don't want you all in our business because "we're grown"
yet, at the same time we flip out when we hear you say
"I'm a grown ass man" because somehow that's different to us
we say we don't want to be your mothers
when you start expecting us to cook, clean and baby you when
you're sick
but we fail to remember we did
all that and more when we were trying to "catch" you
but stopped when we thought we "had" you
we get comfortable
start sleeping in oversized sweats, holy t-shirts and thick socks
putting pink sponge rollers in our hair or wrapping it and throwing
on a scarf
but still expect you to tell us how sexy we look at night
no wonder we fight all the time
female poets like myself tend to get up on this mic and vent
will talk time after time about failed relationships
sleepless nights, tear stained pillows and "niggas who ain't shit"
and in all honesty, men,
you MUST be tired of hearing it
half the time when you come here
you're probably trying to escape the relationship drama in your

own lives
and you probably ignore
most of the women who step up here
because you already think you know what's going to come out of
our mouths
so I'm trying to be honest here
I won't justify or explain away our wrongdoings
because sometimes,
we are simply not the "great women" we claim to be
but we hope you love us anyway
we fuck up just as much as we say you do
we just think we're slicker about it
can talk our way out of the messiest of situations
with tears
while throwing something you did in the past back in your face
to divert attention away from our own deed
we wear tight clothing, make-up and high heels
in hopes we can grab your attention
but if you approach us and we don't think you're attractive
we say we dressed like that just to make ourselves feel good
we are oftentimes insecure about our bodies
but cover that up by talking shit in front of you about other women
gentlemen, we are so imperfect it's not even funny
but sometimes, in my attempt to build us up
I inadvertently tear you down
and I'm wrong for that

so, to the women who stand up
when I "male bash" men who don't amount to shit
I ask you are you willing to stand up to admit
if you've ever been wrong
to admit all men aren't bad
to admit we have our faults
and to the men don't stand up because you feel like
women don't own up to their own shit
who feel shortchanged and shut down and disrespected
this is for you
I ask you all to please stand
ladies, reach out and grab the hand of the closest man
and repeat after me:
"I'm flawed"
"I make mistakes"
"I'm not perfect"
"I apologize"
and on behalf of every woman who has ever related
to anything I have ever said in one of my poems
I hope you forgive us…

Change

If I could turn back the hands of time
I would have never let you put your penis inside me
because in all honesty
you were not worthy
today's generation takes the concept of sex too lightly
it's almost as if we believe
we're invincible
supposed to get smarter as we get older
but we damn near go backwards instead
ladies-
think about the last 3 men you let slide between your thighs
would you have wanted any of them to father your child?
if not, why were they chosen to enter your sanctuary?
safe sex is only so safe so why are we still playing ourselves
stop getting mad when his face doesn't light up at the notion
of you carrying his seed
when you knew damn well you were the rebound chick
so you trot off to the clinic to terminate what you knowingly
helped create
men-
don't think you're exempt
think about the last 3 women you put your penis inside of
were they worthy of bearing children who will carry your name?
and to think, you have the nerve to be surprised
when she gets upset at your lack of parental capabilities
you came inside her by choice

got "caught up" in the feeling
the moment
the notion of pussy being more powerful than your self-control
so really, how can anybody be mad at anyone else
we are a careless group of people
allowing alcohol and lust to be justifiable excuses
then we wake up the next morning
on top of sheets that smell like sin warmed over
swearing we'll never drink again
promising we won't make the same mistakes twice
but we do
because somewhere along the line we told ourselves
we are the exceptions to the rule
when the truth is we are liars
trying to lessen the blows that reality brings to light
trying to make allowances
for what never should have occurred in the first place
so when does it end
when every educated woman has been reduced to not much more than
the next nigga's baby mama?
when casual conversations at the campus library
revolve around the cost of diapers and formula rather than
textbooks and tuition
since baby daddies ain't shit these days
when young men are taking public transportation to work
since the judge suspended their license

for not paying for the needs of the children they helped
bring into this world
before you open your mouths to refute my points
or even attempt to call me a hypocrite
understand that I'll be the first one to call myself out
the first to say I should have
kept my eyes open
mouth closed
legs shut tight
rather than allowing some men who now
make me throw up a little inside my mouth
at the mere thought of them
to enter my body
so why would I want others to make the same ill-informed choices
I made
I am no better than the next woman yet every day I'm striving to
be
I don't put myself on a pedestal and I'm not always the best role
model
but the difference between myself and many others
is I can admit that
I thought I wrote the game but fell victim to it myself
so I stand before you now
ready and willing to make some necessary changes
and hoping you'll follow suit
listen closely:
African Americans in Alameda County

represent 63% of the counties AIDS cases

but only 13% of the population

3 out of every 4 African American babies

are being born out of wedlock

women are using abortions as

second thought birth control methods

as though vacuuming out your womb

to rid yourself of a growing fetus

is as easy as cleaning the carpet on your living room floor

it has to stop at some point

we have to respect ourselves

our lives

our bodies

otherwise all we will one day be

is empty shells of our former selves

asking ourselves if all this was really worth it

it's time to stop searching in our pockets for change

and start creating some instead

Fill In The Blank

You're kinda cute for a
"fill in the blank"
big girl/skinny girl/short girl/tall girl
just had a baby girl
I want you to have my baby girl
dark skinned girl
must be mixed girl
why can't I just be a cute girl?
not fishing for compliments
so I don't expect you to give them
but when you do
why can't they just be clear-cut
like:
'you're cute'
anything added to that is like
an addendum to a memo-
I've already forgotten the original point of what you said
that 'cute' remark slid right over my head
because now I'm scratching my head
trying to figure out what a
big/skinny/short/tall/dark/mixed girl
is supposed to look like
see you only see what I allow you to
and that's the outer image I've chosen to put on display
and if by seeing just that you still open your mouth to say
I'm cute for a

"fill in the blank"
how would you react to my hidden flaws
stretch marks
each line defined by the human beings
I gave life to
extra skin around my midsection
disguised by large belts
so I don't have to walking around sucking in
skin a little too dry
because I showered and dressed in a rush
without putting on lotion
since I had about 20 minutes to get to
a job I was already running late for
no lunch for the day because my last bit of change
was put in the meter
so I could sit at my desk hoping
quarters counting for 8 minutes each
would prevent me from getting
yet another parking ticket
see, I am imperfect
which means we are imperfect
because I am my sister's keeper
but we try to keep our flaws neatly tucked away beneath
practiced smiles
and carefully hidden extra folds of brown skin
but we feel like we've failed miserably when you say
we're cute for a

"fill in the blank"

see we were hoping you would have to wear sunglasses around us

because the radiance that emanates from our melanin filled skin

is almost blinding

hoping you would peer into pupils doubling as our soul's windows

waiting for you to notice how each strand of our

natural/braided/permed/weaved/coarse/straight/dark hued hair

represents a hardship that we have overcome

we want you to look closer

dig deeper

search beyond what's glaringly apparent to you

and see us as just cute

so the next time your lips are fixed to say

you're cute for a

"fill in the blank"

save your breath

because half-assed compliments will be treated the same as

none at all

Get It Together

Too many women are searching for a man to complete them
when they should be looking for a partner to complement
their fully formed beings
but somewhere in between generations
we've forgotten our roles
become the aggressors
the initiators
expecting when we should be accepting of the fact that
everything happens the way it's supposed to
ladies:
there are few things men dislike more than an insecure woman
and too many of us wear our insecurities like
badges of honor rather than cloaks of shame
never taking the time to realize
he has already glimpsed the flaws
we've tried so hard to cover up
he's just sticking around until
another option shows up
and how can we blame him
we will down talk another woman in a second
make proclamations like
'you can't name five women prettier than me'
or 'she know she ain't got shit on me'
or 'is it my fault her man wants me'
never stopping to think that men overhear these comments
and immediately stop taking us seriously

because if we were happy/comfortable/content
with we
then we wouldn't be concerned about she
but we're not, so we are
and this is why half of today's relationships
don't go very far
a man will only do what you allow him to
yet a man will never do what you try to force him to
we stopped playing our positions
not in the sense of being cowered into submission
but in recognizing the term 'women'
came with an original definition
to be a man's companion
his partner
an extension of his being
yet change over time has us doing stupid shit like singing
songs about putting a ring on it
so what he's supposed to propose to you
because you brag about what the next man could do?
shouting about your independence
but conveniently forgetting
your wallet whenever a bill arrives at the table
but we want to show him we're ready, able and stable
that we can hold our own, take care of ourselves
but when he gets in the shower
we're running to check his cell
because we never quite believe we're enough for him

convincing ourselves that every other woman wants him
and he'll be too weak to resist temptation
when really, we're too self conscious to allow ourselves to think
what we bring to the table is sufficient
when will we get it together
if I'm a spokesperson for you ladies when I'm speaking about
the men who ain't shit
then let me be the front runner
when too many of you have remained silent
when you're not quite ready to admit
you're not always right, don't know everything
he's not your father/ex man/or ex best friend
more like someone you should try to let in
ladies-
we have to get it together, come together, be better together
or that man you once thought would wait around forever
will disappear in search of someone better
all because you were never
good enough
for you

Her Worth

You say she's good enough to sleep with
but not enough to be with
loosely translated
she can get the penis but not the title
so now I'm confused
because when I read between the lines
I see that you're willing to subject yourself
to the possibilities of numerous STD's
and unwanted pregnancies
for women you wouldn't even introduce
to your families
and all for what
a quick nut?
yet another woman you've told to
keep it on the hush
because you don't want anybody in your business
but when she wants to talk to your boy it's all bad
because you told him she gave you the business
so now in more ways than one
she's been fucked
you gave her a disclaimer
told her from day 1 you didn't want to be
in a relationship
yet now she thinks you're full of shit
because your actions don't add up to your words
casual encounters turned into her cooking you dinner

just because

booty calls got extended when you showed up
with an overnight bag
after sex activities started including
pillow talk with soft jazz playing in the background
but you say she's wrong for falling for you
miscommunication?
or careful deliberation?
and you want to know if she'll get up
and cook you eggs in the morning
the better question is
what would you be willing to do?
would you roll off the wet spot
out of the bed of the woman who was only
good enough to dick down
and cook her an omelet
like your name is Larenz Tate?
the answer is 'no'
no, because in doing so expectations would be created
and if there's one thing too many men hate
it's being expected to do shit
it doesn't matter that she opened up her legs
and let you hit
you'll respond to her texts
when you feel like it
show up when it's convenient
take her out when it can be fit

into your schedule
because the category you placed her in
only allows for so much wiggle room
yet and still
you let your emotions get the best of you
when she tells you she's sleeping with
someone else
you become territorial
start claiming her body parts as your own
even though you have no interest in
claiming her as your own
she's a ripper/runner/hoe
for giving away what she's been giving to you
yet she's doing the same thing
you've chosen to do
so what does that make you?
you say you're not
looking for/interested in/ready to make
a commitment
either you're too busy leaving 80
for that 20%
or you need to get your money straight
before you can provide for her
or there's just too much available pussy
roaming the streets
for you to only insert your penis inside one
but we're supposed to understand

play our roles
and if one day your mind changes about "our status"
we're supposed to go with the flow
well fuck the flow
everybody going with the flow
is why you're her baby daddy instead of her husband
it's why she pretends to be hardcore
because you might walk away if she starts showing
too much emotion
it's why so many women end up in the clinic
for antibiotics and abortions
because everybody is just "going with the flow"
so:
stop claiming you're keepin it 100
when you can't count to 75
remember omissions of the truth
are the same thing as lies
so call me a hater
an angry, bitter, male-bashing, single Black woman
if you want to
but hear this:
don't call my phone at 2am and expect me to answer
don't call yourself being mad when I'm doing me
since you decided that "me" wasn't good enough for "we"
you said we're being "real"
tell me, how many dollars have you dished out
for the morning after pill

bullshit will never cease to exist

but maybe one day you can stop being so full of it

so be careful of what you ask for

and mindful of what you say

next time you find one that's only good enough to fuck

realize it's because men like you

made her that way

Kiss It

You may call us angry Black women
say we have chips on our shoulders
attitudes we need to drop
issues we need to work out
problems we need to solve
you know what we say to that?
FUCK YOU!
we're sick and tired
of trying to be superwoman
done with hoping we can live up to
your unrealistic views of perfection
either we talk too much
or don't have our own thoughts
our hair is too short
our skin is too dark
we're either too small or too tall
feet not pretty enough
no ass at all
nails not manicured
breasts too flat
all skin and bones
or big girl fat
we roll our eyes too hard
we smack our gum too loud
we think we know everything
we're too damn proud

we'll never be trophy wives
we're good for booty call hours
I'm here today to tell you
Black women are reclaiming their power
what gives you the right to judge
ridicule and make us feel low
if you can't accept us with our flaws
we don't want yo ass no mo!
please get rid of the belief
that our lives revolve around you
and if at one time they did
from now on, that's no longer true
this is for all the women who've been
lied to, cheated on or disrespected
the ones who've been hurt beyond repair
the ones who ever loved a man
who pretended to love you back
the ones who put their dreams on hold
to help make his come true
the ones who lost sight of their self-worth
but didn't know how to say "I'm through"
this is for the ones who thought
casual sex would turn into a relationship
the ones who pleased their men to no end
only to find out the next female
was doing the same
for the women who thought

a college degree made them smart
but never educated themselves on reality
for the ones who check his
Facebook wall, text messages, emails and tweets
as a sign of their own insecurities
this is for the women who never thought
they were good enough
the ones who sleep around
in hopes that someone will one day find them worthy
the ones who say "I can't stand females"
when they really wish they had true girl friends
who had their back
I write for all of you
I give you a voice when yours has been
silent for so long
I give you respect
whether you've demanded it or not
I AM you
I am every Black woman
who has taken her earrings off
put her tennis shoes on
and rubbed Vaseline on her face
who's ever snatched somebody's man
and then tried to justify it
who's ever kept giving it up
because she believed that tired ass line
"baby, this is the best I've EVER had"

who's had visions of slashing tires
who's called the next woman a bitch
who's gotten sick and tired of meeting men
who want her to take care of them
who doesn't understand why
he keeps choosing quantity over quality
who can't figure out why he says
he wants to know the real her
yet can't handle her past
I am every Black woman who
didn't know if she could make it
through one more day
Scorpio Blues talked about bitter Black women
and I must admit that sometimes I'm one of them
but hear me out
it's time to let it go
time to make some changes
if your man is all bad
leave his ass
if you're havin a messed up day
put that get 'em outfit on
with the six inch heels
and remind yourself that you still got it
you don't need to get your shit together
because you already got your shit together
so show off
put a spring in your step, a smile on your face

an arch in your back and a switch in your waist
and the next time someone tells you
you're an angry Black woman, do this:
stand up
put one hand in the air
curl 4 fingers down with the middle one left out
gather up all your strength and courage
so there's no confusion or doubt
put your other hand on your hip, let your backbone slip
and with the best display of sass
turn around, look over your shoulder
and tell 'em, "kiss my ass!"

Little Big Girl

There's a thin line between 'thick' and 'fat'
and I'm treading it precariously
I hate sucking in
marks left on my stomach
from jeans that used to fit just a couple weeks ago
full length mirrors are not my friends
I crave brownies
heavy on the chocolate and walnuts
with caramel swirled throughout
can eat half a dozen Winchell's doughnuts
or double chocolate Krispy Kremes
I warm up chunks of cake
so the ice cream can melt on top of it
I feel fat at the mere thought of food
wearing sweats and over-sized t-shirts like
cloaks of shame
500 sit-ups a day and I still hear
"it's okay, after all-you had a baby!"
depressing
creating workouts that never pan out
because I punk out
trying to do it alone
don't tell me I'm dramatic
or that there are others far worse off than me
the thing is, they aren't me
so they have no real meaning to me

I'm not a victim
more like on the cusp of survival
but unable to swing over the edge
it's not about insecurities so much as gross realities
I teared up at the site of
stretch marks on the underside of my arms
pondered whether or not my butt could be too big
worried if my thighs were meaty instead of healthy
elongated my neck in pictures
so it would never look like my chin was doubling
just 10 more pounds
maybe 15
but for every 1 lost it seems like 2 more are gained
and I'm back at square one
leaving top buttons open, buying long shirts
and trying to resist
that last Hershey's kiss

Me to You

I want to write without reservation
free from thinking too deeply about
how my words will be interpreted
how you'll feel about what I
consistently hold back from telling you
I want to yell out loud in the most
silent whisper I can muster
that I don't want to breathe
if I can't inhale the essence that is you
you make me long for endless days
and sleepless nights
languid movements where we both
embrace all that the other is
you have made love evolve into
more than just another four letter word
allowing me to reach out and
grab a hold of feelings
I never thought I was worthy of having
for you I would walk to the
edge of the earth and beyond
knowing that if my time here was to end
I could only hope to come back as a piece of you
you are not perfect
are not flawless
are not some idealistic representation
of what I dream for

more importantly
you are reality
are a real interpretation of
what I want the son I yearn for
to grow up emulating
you make me smile in places
dark clouds once resided
quiet nights when I don't have you by my side
bring about not so distant memories
of kisses that made my lips tremble
and the goose bumps on my shoulders
stand out for all to see
you bring me laughter and tears
and hopes for many years
of blissful content
the corners of my soul turn up
at the mere thought of your existence
I ache for you to cast away your fears of normalcy
in exchange for happiness
that I know only I can bring to you
sometimes I sit and watch you sleep
wondering if I could ever bring about
the peaceful calm that lays like a veil atop your face
wondering if I was to plant
soft and subtle kisses up and down your spine
would you smile in your sleep
if I rubbed your shoulders when you were tense

offered my chest when you were weary
would that be enough
be sufficient
be all that you needed
when I'm awake, my thoughts are of you
when I'm asleep, my dreams
are filled with visions of our togetherness
I don't usually write love poems
more like real poems
but that love that envelops me
like a thick haze on a humid day
made me put pen to pad
to get out all I have to say
I   Love   You
I'm not shying away from the truth
not finding ways to make it sound
any less real than it really is
I've fallen so deep in you
that no part of me would be honest and true
if I didn't express it now
every song I hear brings lines to mind
that assist in defining my emotions
every pearl of wisdom I receive
has allowed me to believe
that I speak the words
most are afraid to say
yesterday I loved you

today I love you
tomorrow is not guaranteed
but if it were, I'd love you still
if you pulled apart the layers
of my heart
you would see that it beats
in synchronicity with yours
while still being my own person
I long to be the extension of you
wanting my steps to match yours
my eyes to reflect yours
with you, my pride no longer matters
my ego no longer exists
and I stand on the tallest of buildings
and the highest of mountains
and the tops of trees
for all the world to see
for everyone to know-
you had me at hello…

Thirsty

I thought you offered to buy me a drink
because I was thirsty
not because you were thirsty
and planned to follow me around the club
for the remainder of the night
I'm a little confused
because I was under the impression
that you were just being a gentleman
not that after my $10 drink was set down
on the bar
you would go so far
as to not only ask for my name and number
but where I live, do I have kids
what's my sign and bust line
how many friends do I have for your friends
do I have a man
and if so can you just "be my friend"
what the fuck
I can't win
if I turn down the drink
then supposedly I think I'm too good for it
one of those "independent bitches"
who don't need a man for shit
but if I accept it
it's like I signed a contract that doesn't expire
until 2am

and in between now and then
I'm not allowed to talk to any other men
because in some unwritten handbook
that drink is like a ring on my finger—
a binding agreement
so nowadays women really have to think
about shit like this
in our minds, it's simple etiquette
you ask, I accept, express appreciation, then step
but now there's a disconnect
because you think acceptance means interest
if all you wanted was to get at me
you didn't need to try to impress me
try to entice me with liquid concoctions
all the while knowing that with inebriation
comes alleviation of all common sense
but maybe this just applies to the new boys type of
generation of men
if buying a woman a drink is the chivalrous thing to do
with no strings, expectations or high hopes
then cool
but if your intent is to convince me to exchange
skin for shots
keep your $10
hell, don't even point out the bottle
because women don't have any obligation to strangers
who offer false promises in cocktail glasses

so before you motion to the bartender

that you "got this"

understand-

you don't "have this"

a drink won't "get you this"

and the most I can promise

is a smile

a sincere thank you

and genuine appreciation

for you quenching

my thirst

Not The One

Every man you meet/date/kiss
is not "the one"
so why do you keep getting broken hearts
maybe because you wear yours on your sleeve
for the world to see
but, that will get you nowhere in a hurry
see, apparently you were absent
for the self-worthy conversations growing up
didn't learn that men come a dime a dozen
and if you open yourself up
to that 10 out of 12
then 9 times out of 10
you will disappointed
yet only have yourself to blame
you knew the minute he came
then crawled from between your legs
without so much as a defined commitment
to see you again
that he was not "the one"
you knew when he
verbally disrespected the woman who gave him life
that he could never respect you
and so he was not "the one"
when he denied fathering his ex's child
by proclaiming he "knew" he pulled out in time
it was obvious that he was not "the one"

yet over and over again you have allowed these men
to get beneath your skin
between your thighs
permeate your mind with thinly disguised lies
and then you get hurt when it's over before it even began
when you realize his heart was never in
your physical situation
and your connection only lasted
as longs as he could hold out before ejaculation
you knew better yet didn't do better
and now your heart hurts
pride is worn down
ego is shot
each time one of them slips through your grasp
and you're forced to start all over again
if this cycle doesn't end you'll be nothing more to men
than a chick that got ran up in by him and his friends
since six degrees of separation is more like two these days
in the Bay
and even though you're looking for ways to be discreet
people always know your business
and it sucks
because half the time
half of these men
aren't worth half the effort you put into them
so you get half-assed relationships
where they won't meet you halfway

yet at the end of the day you're still grasping for things to say

to get them to stay

but they won't

because if their intentions from the beginning

were honest and true

they would not continue to leave you as they do

so open your eyes

close your legs

put an under construction sign on your emotions

and an arm's length distance

between you and the next man

who comes through that revolving door

you

yes, you

I'm talking to you

and your friend/cousin/sister/daughter

but most importantly

to the you I see

in the mirror's reflection

looking back at me....

Single Mother Speaks

I change diapers countless times every day
pour cups of juice that stain my carpet
find cookie crumbs between my sheets
brush teeny tiny teeth
and watch the Elmo movie over and over
with my daughter
by myself
and sometimes it's overwhelming
see, he merged with me
and I carried she
so we were 3
he, she and me
but he left me
so in a sense he left she
and now there's no more him and me
no more we
just me and she
and sometimes I get angry
look at her and wonder if he
loves/misses/craves/yearns for kisses
on the eyelids from our creation
then I hear her voice say
"I'm mommy's best friend"
and I get protective
can't fake an ounce of respect for
men who shirk their responsibilities

and I'm not just talking about money
us mothers will do whatever we have to
to make sure our child doesn't go without
but how can we explain to
miniature versions of us
that no amount of money
will make daddy call our house his home
shhhh…..can you hear that?
it's the sound of yet another teardrop
dripping down her face
as she tries to decide
which bills not to pay
or how to make a way
out of no way
and send her baby to daycare
this shit isn't fair
why won't you be there
you can't separate me from her
so try sitting down
and explaining to us both
how 3 got reduced to 2
due to what's more convenient
for you
I wish I could hate you
but I don't
because every glance at her
is a constant reminder of you

so you are never far from the forefront of my mind
there is no more you and I
which is more than fine
but should I have to ask you to
watch her/visit her/spend a few minutes with her
don't cast blame when she starts
calling you by your first name
or when another man steps up to the plate
in this game
because I refuse to shortchange her
we get accused of being bitter
angry/haters/money hungry/finger snapping/neck rolling
baby mamas
but how would your seeds become children become
young men and women who
don't grow up to make our mistakes
if we don't stand up to make our points
why don't you stand up and make time
make a difference
allow her to revel in your presence
rather than your presents
I'm speaking for mothers who are
too tired/too tried/too worn out
to find energy to speak up for themselves
I'm speaking out for those who love our children
but never chose to raise them alone
I won't tell you to do your job

more like enjoy your blessing

cultivate your creation

step up

or one day, maybe sooner than you think

you will be nothing more

than a distant memory

Text Message

You broke up with me

through a text message

well maybe broke up is a

strong term

since our encounters consisted mainly of

poetry, conversation and great sex

but it still felt like a break up

because my heart leapt out of my body

and shattered into pieces

as I scrolled through my phone

and read the words

you couldn't say to me face to face

or even ear to ear

because I would've preferred to at least hear

that I was being discarded

like yesterday's sports page

I knew what we could never be

yet I was content with what we were

because it was beautiful

sensual

private

and in the back of my mind

I kind of hoped each time

would've been like the first time

and you would press rewind

and keep reminding yourself

that you liked me
I wanted to be more than
sex to you
knew we couldn't go on dates
for fear of what people may say
or even take trips to a
secret place
because we had to play our roles
make sure we didn't stray
but I couldn't stop myself from wondering
what if
and maybe
and possibly I could be
more than just privacy
more than late night trysts
and text message conversations
and poetry
because sometimes even poets get tired of poetry
I just wanted you to want me
and maybe in your own way you did
but I'm sure it wasn't the same as me
sure it didn't have the intensity
that filled up my own emotions
I thought my lips would split
from the smile that I knew
was stretching from ear to ear
each and every time I saw you

would have to remove myself from your presence
in order to slow down my
rapidly beating heart
because my Aries fire
burned brightly for you
but I may as well have been
sending up smoke signals
because to you I was worth
not much more than the two thumbs
you most likely used
to text me that it was over
that we were done
and I had no say so
because you were looking for "the one"
and she couldn't be me
and I took that
internalized that
ran with that
but never let you see my pain
because poets are only supposed to
convey raw emotions on microphones
and in front of crowds
so I'm standing here now
just to say
that I deleted your
hastily texted explanation for
why we can be no more

because I deserve more
than closure through a text message
or maybe
to you
I didn't

The Cycle

Just because a man whispers to you
"let's make a baby"
while you're riding him into oblivion
doesn't mean he really wants you to carry his seed
so why do well allow ourselves to bring more
fatherless children into our community
sex has never equated to love
so how will producing a child
conceived in moments of lust bring about that
happily ever after-2 parent household-white picket fence fantasy
that rarely ever comes true
these days we have
35 year olds becoming premature grandmothers
and babies making babies
all the while not concerned with anything more than
making sure their kids are "fitted"
teenage mothers prancing through local malls
shopping for baby Jordans and baby Roca Wear
instead of baby bottles and babies formula
because it's cute
getting off on "oohs" and "aahs" and
"aww, girl, your backpack matches his diaper bag"
and "don't trip girl, you didn't need his ass anyway"
so the cycle continues
we have little girls growing up without male influences
learning how to "walk it out" before learning how to walk

spelling BET instead of ABC and we laugh
buy them miniature stripper clothes because they fit
thinking it's amusing when they learn to repeat
"this nigga ain't shit"
and fail to correct their man hating mentalities
since their mothers never had a father to teach them any differently
so the cycle continues
we have little boys growing up without male influences
believing at the age of seven that they have to be protectors
struggling with the dichotomy of soft versus hard
not knowing if it's more manly to open a door
or hit with an open hand
running to friends for guidance since
mommy just doesn't have what it takes to raise a man
bedding young girls because their
rapper/actor/idols say it'll make them a man
so the cycle continues
and now we have him and her, he and she
younger versions of you and me playing grown up
attempting to create a product of the two of them
that will ultimately be brought up just like them
we're proclaiming the children are our future
but aren't doing anything to better their present
so what can possibly lay in store for our people
we rely on the misguided school system to
educate our children about sex
yet become enraged when they engage in it

as though anything in our society promotes abstinence
so now we have 13 year old little shay shay
hooking up with 17 year old grown ass jay jay
giving it up in her mother's bed
he told her she wouldn't get pregnant
if he just put the head in
but she already has images of little "thems"
running through her head
and it doesn't matter that jay jay has 3 other kids
she knows he'll give her money if she demands it
so now his presence isn't required
and the cycle continues
I heard of "taking your daughter to work" day
but since when did it become fashionable
to push strollers on junior high campuses
to threaten to take child support out of his
Mickey D's check so you and your baby can have
the latest pair of matching j's
this shit is sick
depressing to watch swollen bellies beneath training bras
young boys sticking and moving
not being taught the responsibility of being a man
so they opt to not waste time trying to raise one
and young women give in
brought up by single mothers themselves so they think it's
no big deal to become one
told repeatedly that men have the option of being fathers

so they don't force it
would rather remain content using EBT cards at the corner store
and their child's name for lines of credit
than birth control to prevent
bringing yet another statistic into our community
the cycle has continued for far too long
it has spiraled out of control and now we
take buses to prison in our church clothes
to show off our kids' new gold ones to jumpsuit clad daddy
we put our 14 year olds on Depo since
"they're just gonna do it anyway"
but don't warn them about the repercussions
and now we have little girls thinking they're ready
to become mothers
because their hymens have been broken
and little boys thinking it's
little girls' fault if they become pregnant
because nobody is telling them the pull out method
was never designed to work in the first place
so the cycle continues
but it doesn't have to
let's start actually communicating truths with our children
tell them more than "keep your pants up and your dress down"
how about something like "spreading your legs won't keep
a REAL man around"
let's try being do-ers instead of say-ers
show-ers instead of tell-ers

if we keep making babies who are making babies

then our babies will never get a chance to be babies

so let's stop while we can

stop before it gets so out of hand that

mothers and daughters are shaking asses at the club together

and dropping it like it's hot

while trading stories about men

in between sharing blunts and shots

for the first time in a long time

let's come together and do something right

something other than gossip and hate and fight

if we care about the future of the

seeds that we produce

then stop teaching these little girls

that young single motherhood is cute

it's time to break the cycle…

B List Rapper

Sometimes I feel like a B-List rapper
knowing some of you would only listen to my words
if I put a recycled beat behind them
and regurgitated tired ass verbs
but my message to the masses is more powerful
than a bootleg cd encased in plastic
so I'm tryin to write books to help elevate your mind
not ask if you mind downloading my latest
sounds just like everybody else's track
it's wack that poets rarely get respect
but mediocre rappers get gold stars and mic checks
I want to make you think
read between my lines, my words, pick apart my verbs
I'm tryin to be heard
without you having to smoke herb
just to "feel me"
this is the "real me"
no glitter no gold and I haven't sold
myself to the concept of selling as many sets
of Dr. Seuss poetry so I can promote me
under the pretense of entertaining you
this shit is not a game and I am not the same
as those who came before or those who will follow
I spit when there's nothing left in me to swallow
what's your reason?
because to me it looks like it's the season

for bullshit

everybody tryin to give their two cents

when they'd be better off depositing it

in the bank of 'who gives a shit'

and I don't give a shit if you think I'm a hater

simply because I'm a lover of me

I mean tell me, does anybody know any words

to any of your songs, other than the hook?

NO

so in my eyes you're a crook

stealing people's attention by disguising dumb shit

as creative bliss

I pisses me off that we're both labeled as artists

because until you come with something designed

to do more than just make fingers snap

in my eyes you're elementary and nothing more than that

and in all honesty I wouldn't want you compared to me

because I'd much rather just be

a poet.

R-I-P

You'll never wife her
never introduce her to the fam as anything more than a friend
because in the back of your mind once she let you in
that was the beginning of the end
she is your personal RIP
R-I-P
you're Running Inside the Pussy at will
and she lets you
not because that's all she wants to be
more like that's all you'll let her be
and she'd rather be a little bit of something
than a whole lot of nothing
so she's settling for being your plaything
you call her your bitch
not as a demeaning term
more like a badge of honor to be worn
beneath the sheets
behind closed doors
she is your whore
and she wears the label with pride
because all she really needs to hear
is that she's yours…sometimes
someway, somehow
she's carved her niche on top of your dick
found her place sitting on your face
she is a rider in every sense of the word

but it's absurd for her to think she'll ever be
more than your little secret
her reputation has gone to shit
thought she was your 'it' girl
demoted to your 'for now' girl
has become nothing more than your 'right here' girl
she is a grown woman calling herself
'Daddy's little girl"
and you love it
don't have to do shit but make her cum quick
and let her believe her name is written all over it
she wants to be so much more
but she's a realist
well aware of the box she's placed herself in
so she's resigned to being only his homie-lover-friend
she's your up close and personal RIP
and at every opportunity
you're
Recklessly Invading her Pussy
she's a RIP
but wishes she was a whole lot more
wants something else out of life than being a casual whore
wants phone calls instead of texts
restaurants instead of take-out
resorts instead of motels
beds instead of stairwells
she wants what you in the midst of your

moans and thrusts and kisses

promise her

but you smile at her

fill her head with false ideologies and grandiose lies

knowing once you're no longer between her thighs

you won't be forced to look in her eyes

and you've survived yet another night

it's not right

but since she'll say it's okay

you'll give a Kanye type of shrug and walk the other way

because after all she knows her role

and she'll continue to play it

while Remaining Involved Privately

as your personal R-I-P

Pretender

If I see one more young Black man standing outside the club
wearing a white t shirt/blue jeans/and Nikes
I will scream
I'm so tired of the 'ay lil mama I'm tryna see what you workin wit'
of being called a bitch because I express my disinterest
or being frustrated out of my mind while trying to find
a clear path to the bathroom
without groping fingers grasping any visible piece of my skin
see
I thought I was in mature environments with mature individuals
with mature intentions and behaving respectfully
yet maybe I was wrong because some of the shit I see
leaves a bad taste in my mouth
like intoxicated men volunteering to go down south
on women they just met at the bar
so she doesn't even know his full name
much less where his mouth has been
yet he expects her to willingly give in
or women who get called hoes because they chose
to step out scantily clothed
yet get offended by the insult
or men with no job, goal or plan
yet claim they wanna be your man
knowin they ain't bringing shit to the table
or women who think their Mac made up looks
are enough to take the place of self-help books

that the teach them the difference between
being a girl and a lady
see, my mind is racing faster than I can write or speak
because I'm surrounded by falsities
fake eyelashes/nails/contacts/hair
because she's too self-conscious to be seen naturally bare
fake designer wallets/money clips/cubic zirconia bracelets
because he's too wack to admit he can't afford that real shit
or women whose idea of etiquette
is a man is supposed to pay for things yet she continues to swear by
her independence
bullshit
we are so wrapped up in upholding these images
even when they have nothing to do with the real us
so intent on being somebody we know we aren't
that we lose sight of any individuality we once had
becoming carbon copies of carbon copies
since nobody knows how to be themselves lately
because we think we'd rather be someone else
never knowing they would rather be someone else
so somebody's become nobodies since nobody seems
to know any better
and shit won't get any better if we don't make it
I don't have all the answers
but the niggas and bitches epidemic has spread like cancer
and I want nothing to do with it
so the next time you're with the bullshit

miss me or get dismissed by me
for pretending to be somebody
you're not

Shit

He told you you ain't shit without him
weren't shit before him
wouldn't be shit after him
and you were full of shit if you thought otherwise
so you stayed
simply because you wanted to be the shit
needed to be his "it" girl
his "other hoes ain't got shit on me" girl
his "I'll beat a bitch ass over my nigga" girl
all the while failing to realize
you're still just a little girl playing grown up
caught up in show and tell
showing and proving you're his down ass chick
fuck his bottom bitch
she ain't got shit on you
doesn't matter that he has no 9-5
or that he's up and out from sunset to sunrise
cuz he's just bein a man and you're part of his master plan
and it's hard out here for a pimp
while you're struggling to pay his bills like a simp
see, you say niggas ain't shit
but exclude your man from that category
then turn around and say
"my nigga can't do shit without me"
so maybe you're really the nigga in the relationship

and he's the bitch

since to hear you tell it you run this shit

that was right before you dropped to your knees

when he commanded you to suck it

you justifying your actions by saying it's your dick

but to him you're just another chick swingin on it

got him dropping you off at work like his name is Jody

so everybody can see your man

chauffeuring you in your car

that you gave him gas money to fill up

you keep killing his seeds since he said he never wants kids

yet keeps cumming inside you

but never goes with you to the clinic

a leather belt is on deck as a threat

because to him you're like a child who should be kept in check

should cook, clean, and get dressed up

whenever he wants to show you off

as the possession you've shown yourself to be

and that's not okay with me

because I'm tired of your tears

tired of watching your wasted months turn into years

because you can do better/did better/were better/are better

than the shell of your former self that is before me

but the 'you' that you see isn't the same as me

so you settle for what's given by he and I can't let this shit ride anymore

I'm not tryin to save you because you don't think you're lost

can't lead you down a road when you're not ready to follow
you can only preach on so many Sundays to a 6 day sinner
before you have to let them find their own way
so no, I'm not your savior
I'm just someone who cares
someone who sees you're stripping yourself bare
but leave you alone because you're grown, right?
yet a grown ass woman shouldn't be told by her man
that she betta learn to act right or he's gone
never thinking maybe you'd be better off alone
because you say he completes you
in the back of your mind you weren't a whole woman
until he came through
he brings plenty to the table
good dick with only the occasional STD
girls who call your phone just to breathe
empty condom wrappers in the pockets of his jeans
but you don't need me to save you
since captain saved a hoe a long time ago
so maybe I'll leave you be
create a little distance between you and me
because my heart hurts to see a young woman
destroying herself emotionally, piece by piece
I could tell you you're worth more than this
and that you're beautiful and stronger than you realize
but wise words fall on deaf ears
when they're not ready to hear

so from now on when you tell me he's the one and this is it

I'll just smile and nod and not say shit

because what's apparent right now is this:

most of the niggas wrote me off as an emotional bitch

when they heard me first say niggas ain't shit

when in all actuality it's niggas like you

that this shit applies to

Beautifully Black

In the past I've spoken on
the Black Woman and all she's become
and all she's been
but now I've chosen to take the viewpoint
of an outsider looking in
so sit back and open your mind
because in doing so you'll find
that I've decided to take a stand
regarding today's Black Man
I'm not an expert but I'll speak on what I can
he comes in different forms
different hues and different shades
a variety of shapes and sizes
the essence of man is what he portrays
from the moment he was born
he began preparing for survival
armed with faith, hope and trust
relying on instinct and the Bible
he was taught early on
to provide for his wife and seed
but no one told him what to do
when his heart began to bleed
and he was suddenly unable to read
the unwritten laws
of there no longer being a need
for his particular type of breed

in today's society
can he get a beat?
some dap
a pound for the cause
for the life of him
he can't figure out when
his dreams got put on pause
when history turned into the present and
forced him to search for answers
at the bottom of the bottle
and the end of the glass pope
and the tip of the Black
so now there's no turning back
see his pride has been shattered
by the one down below
who's feeding him sin after sin
and then watching him grow
into America's most wanted
and America's greatest nightmare
when in all honesty he's what America
wouldn't dare to put out there
he's a replica of what our great country
is and always will be
all the turmoil built up within him
has made him a product of his society
now let me tell you just what I see:
I see people complaining

about his jeans hanging too low
and his earring in his ear
and his lackadaisical attitude that makes you
want to push him away and keep him near
and the nonchalant air about him
that seems to follow him throughout his days
but even with these minor flaws
I've chosen to sit here and count the ways
the Black man still makes my heart
skip a beat today
I believe in his pride
and I'm down for the ride
he'll take me on
because I know he's still riotous and strong
he's been battered and bruised
mis-treated and mis-used
dismissed and dejected
despite the pillars he's erected
of strength
we're so busy complaining that we can't find "Good Black Man"
that we continue to fail to understand
that part of God's master plan
is to accept, not reject
and embrace, not neglect
look around and do more than just
open your eyes
take a moment to understand, to comprehend,

to realize

that the hope for the world will always reside

inside him

in that smooth butterscotch caramel chocolate toffee coffee

colored skin

so once again I'm reaching deep down and within

to admit that an apology is definitely in store

because the black man undoubtedly has

so much more

to offer than what I've given him credit for

for every time I called you a nigga…I'm sorry

for all the occasions I doubted

your sincerity…I'm sorry

for the many languages I've used to tell you

'you ain't shit'…I'm sorry

for the fake numbers I gave you in the club…I'm sorry

for the eye rolling, neck popping,

finger snapping 'Black Girl Attitude'…I'm sorry

for all the nagging and bugging

lack of caressing and rubbing…I'm sorry

no ifs, ands, buts or maybes

I just want to appreciate the gift God gave me

when he made the Black Man

so I'm proud to stand here before you

even if I'm standing alone

to tell you I've matured, I've wised up,

I have grown

when I look at my reflection

I see you in place of me

and I see all the things in history

leading up to what you will one day be

console yourself with these words

with these promises in fact

that no matter what goes down

I will always have your back

I will walk behind you to catch you if you fall

provide the love I know you need

but be your best friend above all

the only thing left to do as I take my final stand

is reach out and grab the hand

of the irresistible, incredible, indescribable

Black Man

Can I Be

As the sweet melody from your
fingers lightly caressing the
black and white keys fills me up
I sit back
close my eyes
and wonder while my thoughts wander
how I have found something
I never knew I was looking for
tell me, where were you when
I was sifting through rubbish
searching for the diamond in the rough
that always seemed out of my reach
can I be your song with no words?
if you compose me and
breathe me in
exhaling will be far from your mind
I shut myself off from the
possibilities of attachment
for fear of broken promises
and unfulfilled desires
but I find myself watching and waiting for you
waiting for you to tell me
what kind of love you're dreaming of
see, I want to be that
exquisite, exuberant
extraordinary, extravagant

exciting, enticing, igniting, delighting

diligent, delicate, decent

but full of imperfections

girl you never really knew

but always wished you did

can the time come when you

like me more than cornbread and cornrows

because the feeling that overcomes me

to the tips of my toes

is overwhelming

while I would like nothing more than

for you to be the missing link

in my chain

the center piece

of the jigsaw puzzle

that makes up the very essence of me

I tell myself to be wary of

things that seem too good to be true

and deny the fact that I could get used

to ribs and links

and kissing against kitchen sinks

and exchanging light embraces

while gazing into each other's faces

as we sit on the rocks

by the dock of the bay

I want you to say yes

when your first instinct is to say no

and let me take the time to hold you so

we can recline in our seats

and peer at the orange moon

constantly chastising time for moving so soon

can I be like your music?

my range of emotions

like the waves of the ocean

brushing up against the shoreline

making every note that you hit

indicative of my soul permeating your mind

I'm that sunshine you rarely find

after the last trail of whispered footprints

fades from the sky

I'm so deep and so real and

so confused about how to feel because

the smile you place upon my face

is enough to erase all doubts

my mind tells me it's too soon to tell

but my heart keeps fluttering

despite all the warning bells

that surround us

can you be the fire to my desire

my reasons

so I can tell you that

if this world were mine

mine would mean ours

and ours would mean we

and 1+1 would equal 1 not 2
and I can see myself being the extension of you
and I'm hesitant to put these
words into play for fear of
repercussions and what you might say
but I can get used to this
although neither of us holds
the key to our coming days
if I were Shakespeare I'd tell you
to let me count the ways
I'm feeling you
and we could take
a long walk around the park
after dark
and we can vibe and flow
and let each other know
that some things are better left unsaid
since staring into my eyes
puts you into my head
whether we're slowing down
or speeding up
or standing still to enjoy the rush
of emotions that flood over us
I'd rather see you than not
be around you than away
be with you than without
at any time of the day

because the words I find myself

so afraid to say

are emanating through my very pores

in hopes that one day

I can be yours

and you won't feel the need

to search for satisfaction from another

and you won't fight the attraction

we feel for each other

so, tell me-

can I be you not-so-secret lover?

your earth, wind and your fire

your pot of gold at the end of the rainbow

when the time comes just let me know

if you will allow yourself to let go

and tell me…

can I be?

That Man

Your strength fills me with pride
makes me want to reach out and touch you
to prove to myself that you are not
a figment of my imagination
you rise everyday determined to
face a society set out to destroy you
since the beginning of time
and I admire that
respect that
even though I don't always show that
you are one of those men women always say
there aren't enough of
so can I hold your hand?
just graze your fingers in anticipation
that you'll take me into the unknown land
and protect me
guide me through the valleys of
fear and discomfort
with the knowledge that we handle things
together
as one
you are brilliant
opening my eyes to a world I
never knew existed
showing me that possibilities are endless
and infinity is a definite probability

we don't have meaningless arguments
more like meaningful debates
about the state of our community
trying to reach back to the unity
that brought you to me
you are beautiful
Colgate smile stretching from ear to eternity
sparkling eyes gazing only at me
I look up to you in wondrous amazement
wishing I could peek into your heart
and just grab hold of a part
because then I will know perfection
you know when to lead and when to follow
I don't have to stroke your ego
only your head after a long day
to show you I'll share your stress with you
I'll put half of your burdens
on my shoulders to bear
because I have your back
I know you have your priorities straight
so I don't mind not being
at the top of your list
just put me somewhere between
the beginning and the end
and I'll fall in line where I fit in
you don't have to call everyday
don't have to send text messages or emails

just because I do
because I'm comfortable with the knowledge
that you care
you walk on the outside
and open doors and pull out chairs
and run your fingers through my hair
and you kiss me in a way that tells me
you're not going anywhere
that lets me know unequivocally
you are all the man I could ever ask for
I'm hoping one day you will
make me your wife
with no "y" at the end of that title
because we're not in high school anymore
you're not afraid to hold my hand in public
because you want the world to see
you have me
when in all honesty, you are the prize
you are what all women wish their guys were
the truth
from head to toe, you are what I dreamt for
even before I went to sleep
I know I can shed tears on your chest
and you won't think I'm less
of a woman
I can ask for you to hold me
and you won't think it's a sign

of my insecurities

you make me want to cook for you

make pancakes from scratch and bake pies

make me vow not to tell you any lies

because you deserve better than that

nothing less than the best

and I'm qualified to be just that

let me give you babies

a whole clan of beautiful you's and me's

who are equipped to carry on the legacy of love

hear me when I tell you this

you are what's right

in a world full of so many wrongs

and if I could carry a tune

I'd put this all in a song

that I'd sing in a roomful of people

only to you

but for now I'll satisfy myself with

stringing these words together

in hopes that you'll catch my drift

your faith enlightens me

your heart welcomes me

your drive empowers me

your presence warms me

and I am the lucky one

too many women say there are no good men

and when they find one

they still find something
wrong with him
and I don't want to be like them
I want them to know it's possible to meet
that man
he may look like the one who did them wrong
may even be someone they knew all along
but hopefully they'll look beneath the layers
and discover his radiance the way
I've discovered yours
I know I'll never have the guts
to tell you all this to your face
so I can only hope that one of these days
I'll be speaking these words on the mic to a hushed crowd
and you will be there
watching…listening….knowing
that you are the man I am speaking of

Calling You Out

Why do people claim to be
grown ass men and women
but still exhibit childish behavior
it's a sickness
walking around pretending to be
something you're not
without realizing how transparent
you really are
I'm calling you out without
saying your names
because you already know
like you…self-proclaimed
proud, righteous Black man
getting off on writing pieces
about snow bunnies
or you…yelling bullshit on the mic
time after time
hoping people will think the
the fact that you're yelling your poem
means you're saying something of substance
or you…believing if you use
intelligent sounding vocabulary in your pieces
people will look beyond the fact
that your poems come straight from
the book "Black History for Dummies-
A Crash Course"

or you…so concerned with how a guy
could possibly not be interested in you
that you spend your time
watching him watch me
so yes, I'm calling you out
because nobody else is
too many of these "poets"
think that they're true artists since
spoken word is freedom of speech
when in all honesty what that means
is you're able to talk
not that you're really saying shit
you get mad when
people continue to talk through your pieces
but haven't stopped to think that maybe
they simply have no desire to
to fake an interest
in what you are saying
you talk about how Black women
should respect themselves and their bodies
but spread your legs for
sweet talking poets
while thinking they couldn't possibly
be talking about your sweetness on the mic
I'm tired of keeping quiet so I'm speaking out
not out of hatred or ill will
but because I'm sick of

so many of you smiling in the faces
of those you stab in the back
or clapping and snapping for people's poems
when you only listened to the first few lines
or standing up to spit
just to get a better view of the female
you hope to take home with you
it's time to grow up
realize a white collar with a button up
has nothing to do with getting
your grown man on
and your pants hanging off your ass
won't get you a second glance
since 'saggin' spelled backwards is 'niggas'
and that's exactly what you will continue to be
if who you are at your core
is the mediocrity I see before me
you think the woman you strive to become
is defined by the
lightness of your skin and the
length of your hair
so you spend your rent money on
makeup by Fashion Fair
and weaves from Durant Square
because you always fall just a little short
when trying to portray something you're not
so be you

short, tall, fat, thin
what you show on the outside
should reflect what lies within
if you're a fake ass individual
stop claiming you "keep it real"
if you open your mouth to talk about it
for a change, attempt to be about it
if you don't like what I have to say
it's because you aren't prepared for honesty
since you're comfortable living in a fantasy
so wake the fuck up
you can attempt to deny
that this poem applies to you if you choose
but you know
so miss me with the smiles
the laughter, the cheers and the claps
don't act like you care about me
when it's the opposite
in fact-
until you can look in the mirror
and be content with what you see
and show everyone what you're really made of
do both of us a favor-
act like you don't know me

False Realities

I love the hell out of real Black men

but I despise niggas

ones who step to us in the clubs with

smooth, baritone voices

intent on enticing women with

tales of their sexual powers

and tongue flicking and licking endeavors

those guys who claim they

don't want a gold digger

but buy her what she wants to

ensure she doesn't leave

and wonders why she continues to hold her hands out

the ones who can't seem to understand

why a woman doesn't want a

"don't have" man

you "don't have" a car

or "don't have" a job

or "don't have" a place to live

the ones who boast of that AA degree

it took them 4 years to get from Laney

because as I was once told

"our people put too much emphasis on

education as it is"

the ones who call me sista, love, queen

and everything in between

but I'm a bitch if I don't give up my number

a stuck up hoe if I refuse to go down under

but you steady claim "you respect me"

the ones who ask if I can write about

the Black men just trying to make it

the ones who hustle in the streets

because the white men won't hire them

the ones writing

"please baby hold it down for me"

letters from behind bars

the ones who "have to" smoke weed since it

takes their minds off the bullshit they're "forced to deal with"

the ones still fuckin' their baby mama

so she doesn't file for child support

the ones in their grandmother's basement

playing Madden at age 25

watching their lives fade away

as time passes them by

since life just ain't fair for Black men these days

you want me to be nice

give props…give credit

sure, there are guys out there doing right

the ones wifing strong, Black women

but getting head from White girls at night

and you want me to write for you

you, who doesn't give me a second look

when I rock

a ponytail, baggy jeans and oversized shirt

but let me come in a dress and heels and your

feelings get hurt

if I ignore you

you, who says you respect the Black woman

based on her strength and class

bur were seen right outside exclaiming

"damn, that bitch got ass!"

yea, YOU

now as a Black woman

I know we are not all perfect

full of flaws and imperfections we try

every day to patch up

but don't take that to mean

we want a broken ass man

knowing we can do bad all by ourselves

we have taken our dignity down off the shelves

you threw it on

and stepped back into our rightful places

we DON'T need you

but we want you

we CAN live without you

but we choose not to

you DON'T complete us

but you add onto our already formed beings

we may have been created from your rib

but you are born and re-born from our wombs

and look to us to be your backbones

so who needs who?

who relies on who?

from cooking to cleaning, driving and washing

pulling both of us up by my own bootstraps

I'll be damned if I continue to sit back

and watch your fake ass minstrel act

so take note:

I love Black men

from the depths of my soul

to the tips of my toes

but I am NOT your skank, slut, bitch or hoe

I will not let you "beat it up"

and you will not get to "eat it up"

just because you say you're good at it

my role is not to serve you

I don't strive to reach your level

because in so many cases I've already surpassed you

strong-willed, intelligent, educated and wise

Black men, the bar I've set will continue to rise

I'm not a hater, not a basher, not angry

yet and still

I wouldn't be doing these Black women justice

if I didn't speak on the real

so while you engage in debates

about what size ass is your type

know that I stand here calling you out

AY NIGGAS- GET ON MY HYPE!

Break Up No Make Up

You don't really want to be my friend
so stop frontin'
don't act like we can be platonic
hang out on weekends
playing cards and talking shit
while pretending like we don't remember
don't remember the
touching/teasing/tasting/pleasing
feeling/kissing/healing/
missing you whenever we were apart
the hours spent talking about
endless possibilities
of maybe's and we'll see's and
hopefully's
hopeful that tomorrow and the next day
will bring about a closer you and me
but now they won't
now they can't so I
recant my statements about
togetherness and I
recount the number of hours spent
thinking about you
thinking about being in your arms
while you were laid up in her arms
so now I'm up in arms
wondering if half-truths disguised

are the same thing as lies
and how could my eyes have been closed
ears plugged
your mouth was moving too fast so I
wasn't really seeing or hearing you
for all that you really were
or weren't
I mean, is it cheating if I wasn't technically
your woman?
and if the answer is no
then help me figure out
why I feel so betrayed
so played
when I didn't realize I was in the midst
of a game
it sounds lame but I
would've been more prepared
more aware of reality
rather than living in a fantasy
I didn't even know existed
so what now
what's happens next
do I go back to a time
before you were you in relation to me
do I forgive and forget
get moving forward and on
onward with my present and

leave you in my past
do I detest the thought of you
alone or with another
even if I've moved on to
the next brother
simply because you aren't mine
weren't mine
will never be mine
and maybe this whole situation
only existed in my mind
maybe I'll wake up to find
it really was the way
I was told it was defined
because it never was the way
I thought it was defined
it had no concrete definition
just momentary repetition
that left me repeating phrases like
if this world were mine
then at the end of time
I would find you waiting for me
but you won't be there
so now I stare blankly at you
when you say "let's be friends"
it's like you're telling me
"let's take 6 steps back and pretend"
but I'm done with that

finished rehashing that
after I typed the last letter
in the last text message
that signified my last time
initiating contact with you
so let me step back
walk away
retreat from memories that
need to remain just that
and enlighten myself with this truth
I came in this world alone
and will leave it the same way
the footprints you left a trail of
across my soul will fade
minds have been made up
time's up and I'm
letting you watch me from the backside as I
slip and slide right out of your life
back into that of my own
I'm grown
I'll bounce back, snap back
get it together and that's that
but next week, next month, next year
don't come crawling back
trying to get back
because I'm not having that
you had your chance to right your wrongs

but instead chose to sing that tired ass song

about just being friends

give it up- this is the end

the final destination

the road stops, so

pack up shop, jump ship

and don't waste your breath

with anymore of that

we can be friends bullshit…

I'm gone!

Always Crying

Black Women are crying
beneath all our Mac make-up and
processed hair
our enhanced breasts and
dramatic flair
we are crying silent tears
as they slowly make their way
through the cracks and crevices
in our hearts
moistening the flesh-colored
bandages we've used to cover up a part
of our pain
we tell ourselves the salty liquid
is, and will forever be, in vain
for as time has gone by
we have slandered and slain
our own images
our legacy was discarded
somewhere in between
proclaiming 'Black is Beautiful'
and purchasing skin-lightening creams
from reading about a deferred dream
to becoming a P.I.M.P.'s "Queen"
we have become fiends
addicted to the notion that
"assimilation" somehow means "acceptance"

we decided if you're gonna call us
hoes and bitches
we'll use those titles to go from
rags to riches
we'll let a Black man get on
national television and fasten
leashes around our throats
not seeing the similarity
between that and strange fruit
swaying from trees
leashes becoming modern day ropes
we've become the
"Queen B's," the Baddest Bitches
our notoriety goes far and wide
everyone tunes in to urban videos
almost religiously
to see our asses shake from
side to side
we feel such a sense of pride
when allowed to get in the
back seat of some athlete's ride
smilin' and profilin' for those
"unlucky hoes"
while we're still cryin' on the inside
but it's cool, we're satisfied
as long as you can work out
our necks and our backs with your

magic stick
and we can play show-and-tell
when asked, "how many licks"
we can toot it and boot it
and claim it makes us happy
covering pupils with aviator glasses
so we aren't forced to see
the blatant reality that
Black Women are crying
but these days we're simply tired of trying
to act like everything's okay
tired of biting our tongues
when what we really want to say
is listen
listen to what's behind
the words that we speak
and the lives that we lead
and the burdens we bear
and act like you care
enough to find out the reason
behind why we are crying
we are brought up to pretend
that we're hardened within
and content with discarding business suits
in favor of showing more skin
we get drunk and get high
to show we're down to ride or die

and spend our days acting like
we're satisfied "just getting by"
and then we try
to alert you with our silent screams
that at one point
each and every one of us had dreams
although it may seem
that our eyes no longer
have that gleam
the truth is we no longer
want to play on the team
of misunderstandings
I'm a representative of that
double minority
that triple threat
the one you fear the most
but desire the hardest
the one you love to hate
but hate to love
and as a result of us hiding our truths
downplaying our angst
putting everyone else before us
day after day
I fear you will never be the one
to offer even a crumb of an explanation
for the role you've played in why
Black Women are always crying

Deep

Some people tell me that I'm too deep
they say I can be too serious
and I should lighten up from time to time
so as I sat down with a pen and a
piece of paper
I told myself that I would
write something funny
something everyone could laugh at
something to disguise the problems facing
today's society
see, Black people always use humor
from Richard Pryor to Bill Cosby
Katt Williams to Kevin Hart
we use it to mask our real emotions
and hide our true feelings
we'll laugh to ourselves as we write bad checks
calculating how many days it will take the bank
to figure it out
we'll laugh at the bill collectors
who call us from blocked numbers
thanking AT&T every day for Caller ID
we'll laugh at the people who work at McDonalds
and hand us the French fries we plan to eat
while standing in line at "the welfare"
demanding to know why it's taking so long for
"our" money to come

we'll laugh at the people who wear
Payless Shoe Source instead of Nikes and
too small jeans they try to pass off as capris
we'll laugh our way onto Maury
to get our 2nd and 3rd DNA tests done
see, we're willing to laugh at anything
as long as we don't let ourselves travel
to the root of the problem
I can't help but be deep!
as a Black woman, it is simply not in me
to be shallow
I see too many no's that need to be yes's
too many wrong's that need to be righted
too many can'ts that need to be can's
too many won'ts that need to be will's
and I refuse to allow myself to bypass reality
in search of something to make you smile
but, I'll make a deal with you
I'm willing to compromise
I'll speak on something amusing
if you will do the following:
stop buying yourself Jordans
instead of diapers for your baby
stop asking your girl to put
money on your books
stop smoking weed outside the church
stop thinking you're gonna meet your

soul mate on Twitter

stop putting $2 worth of gas in your tank

then getting mad when your car stops

down the street

stop pointing the finger of blame

without realizing how many fingers

are pointing back at you

stop finding God only

after you've committed a crime

stop putting the strength of your man's word

before that of your child

stop buying bootleg DVD's

instead of box office tickets to support

Black actors and actresses

stop using ADD as an excuse

for not having your GED

stop calling Black women "queens"

if the word "bitch" is still a part of your everyday vocabulary

stop selling the drugs that contribute to the genocide of the Black community

stop killing the blessings in your womb simply because

it's not the right time

because, let's be real, there never IS a right time

stop hoping your lips will thin out, your hair will magically

straighten, your booty will plump up, your stomach will flatten, and

the next Rookie of The Year will be your future "baby daddy"

but most importantly

stop laughing away your

misfortunes and indiscretions

your anger and turmoil

your pain and suffering

if you can do this

then I'll gladly slap on a smile

with a ton of white paint to

enhance my already thick lips

and rub a fair amount of coal on my

already Black face

and dance a little jig that will

leave you in stitches

but the actuality of the situation is that

you won't hold up your end of the bargain

and I will continue to be forced to stand before you

as the voice of reason

hoping to make you realize that

the comedic value we associate with our people

does nothing to eliminate the issues

and eradicate the problems

so let's start laughing our way into

careers instead of jobs

into salaries instead of wages

into houses instead of projects

when people tell me I'm too deep

I tell them to utilize each of their 5 senses:

HEAR the gunshots outside your window

TOUCH the bruises caused by an angry blow

SEE the 14 year old stabbed in a playground fight

SMELL the corpse of Anytown USA's next homicide victim

TASTE the filth the man living in the alley eats for dinner

are you feeling me?

or are you too anxious to get home

and watch those late-night re-runs of

Jay Jay and Jackee' and George and Weezy

as you remember Good Times

spent on 227

while imagining you're Movin' On Up

in the midst of standing still

it saddens me that I can't

wrap this poem

this piece of knowledge up

like a carefully boxed gift

but life isn't about pretty bows

and colorful tissue paper

and I'm not about to sugarcoat the truth

I'm gonna remain as deep as I possibly can

as serious as I can stand to be

so forgive me if I don't end this on a

note that's "dy-no-mite"

but I can't see myself

making light

of my people's plight

My People

Something is terribly wrong with my people
as time has gone by
seconds passing into minutes into hours, days, weeks, months, years
we've forgotten our self-worth
we've lost sight of the history of our ancestry
like Ise Lyfe said, we stopped fighting for freedom
and became dumb for free
we stopped using the word "we" and began saying "me"
we started closing our eyes to reality
and stopped believing in what we can be
we are a lost race
we get so caught up in listening to all that we're told
thinking they're actually giving us the Truth
as we grow from young to old
but why would they
why should they when we remain content with the
minute amount of energy they've spent
feeding us gift-wrapped lies
fabrications wrapped in decorations proclaiming declarations of somebody's story
it must be his-story because in my story
they may have come up with the bulb
but my people invented the filament
even so, the light switch in our brains stays off
so we remain in the dark

thinking our skin color renders us
hopeless
incompetent
incapable of being more than just able bodies
so we fall into the abyss of that
hole marked "stupid shit"
and name our offspring after alcohol and cars
and drink our kool-aid out of jelly jars
and rep our cities, our hoods, our blocks
and not so discreetly sell pregnant women
vial after vial of crack rock
I thought I told you that we won't stop
'cause we spout the word found in
newspapers hot off the press
and we love to show the world that
we know how to dress
parading up and down the street
in all those expensive clothes
when we can't afford to pay rent
and our babies have to have WIC
and we're accepting food stamps for
turning tricks and sucking…
the very breath out of our souls
leaving open, gaping holes
where our conscience used to grow
what have we resorted to?
sure, racism has yet to be erased

but it's past time we've moved forward
away from that disparaging reality
instead of giving them the opportunity
to take mental images of you and me
and feed them stereotypically
to the rest of this brain-washed society
we've gotten to the point where
the word "ignorant" defines too many of us
we still insist on sitting
in the back of the bus
and let our hopes for love be overshadowed
by our desires for lust
and then we proclaim
"in God we trust"
we pray at night at our discretion
for admiration and affection
rather than guidance and direction
and wonder why we're being ignored
we claim to be saved
but we still get high, high, high every day
losing sight of the future price
we'll all have to pay
every time we make that choice to lay
in the corrupted beds we make
but then we shrug off with nonchalance
all our needs in favor of wants
and wonder why our aborted seeds

continue to haunt our dreams
or so it seems
it seems like every day
I'm hearing stories of our people slain
their aggressors attempting to gain
ghetto fame
by the status they've attained
by the gunshot wounds marring their flesh
we speak in jest of
getting our children dressed
to visit Daddy in jail
'cause we couldn't afford bail
since we had to get our nails
done
do we think it's fun
to repeat the process with our sons
showing that the cycle of repetition
has only just begun
and we still haven't won
we claim to be down for the cause
but don't care enough about the laws
to vote
although they say we're only
three fifths of a man
we still obligingly stand
for the National Anthem
we're righteous people, am I right?

always ready and willing to fight
for the irrelevant shit we've set our sights on
like supporting energy drinks called
"Pimp Juice"
and spending $175 on the latest pair of shoes
and watching 106th and Park
instead of the 11o'clock news
and thinking the path to Section 8 housing
is one we have to choose
wondering all the while
why we continuously lose
we have our rappers get on TV
wearing crosses hanging down
giving thanks to the one above
but calling out "nigga" to everyone around
that's why they call us clowns
and buffoons
and say we'll never figure out
what the struggle's all about
'cause all we do is scream and shout
about our hoes and bitches
and cars and hood riches
and being ballers and pimps
and walking with that slight limp
as though it adds strength
to our character
is there a remedy for our illness?

or are we supposed to sit in our places and
recline with paper bags encasing bottles of
wine and other liquid poisons
my voice is an endless stream
of soundless noise
as I attempt to throw caution
to our growing girls and boys
I'm not a witness but I can testify
that while time often crawls by
there's not enough of it to waste
so we have to step up and face reality
we're better than
street walkers and drug sellers
alcohol consumers and corner dwellers
although we're brought up to believe
no one race is better than another
we're taught a community always involves
people looking out for one another
so I'm looking out
telling my people we may be lost
but we'll be found
and we'll get up when
we fall down
and we don't all have to be friends
but if we take the time to lend
a helping hand
we'll be playing right into

God's master plan
so color your souls
red, black, green and gold
in honor of this truthful story I just told
pick your hair out
pull your pants up
and raise your fist to the sky
'cause as my people, not as my niggas
we'll get through this by and by

My Poem Speaks

I want this poem to speak for me
I want it to tell the story of
the trials and tribulations
the obstacles overcome
the levels surpassed
the battles fought
the cries of happiness
the tears of pain
the heartache and sorrow
I want this poem
to weave for you the tale of
the young black woman
I want you to testify
to yell out in agreement
to close your eyes
bow your head
slowly nod and wave your hand
in acknowledgement of the validity
of the story this poem is trying to tell
I want the tears to seep out of your hearts
at the thought of a little girl
growing up without a father
never being taught that a man
will only want you for your body
if you fail to present him
with your mind first

I want your eyes to cloud over with
the images of 15, 14, 13 year old mothers
filled with pipe dreams
and the sound of babies' screams
searching for a way to silence
what has turned out to be an expected burden
conception during a moment of
adolescent lust mistaken for love
I want your soul to ache
at the sight of
barbie dolls
bleaching creams
and low-slung 7 jeans
because over and over again
they are constant reminders
that young Black girls
are trying, piece by piece,
to rid themselves of their identities
I want your spine to suddenly straighten
with that jolt of realization
that something is lacking
in the black community
something is not being done
yet, so many of us fail to see
Black man, why is it that your daughter
knows all the words to the
every album by Tunechi or Jay-Z

but can't figure out
the line that comes after
'Lift every voice and sing'
how can she obey these rappers
who convince her it's ok to
shake her ass for cash
but doesn't realize
how it adds to her demise
when she fails to take herself to class?
how does she spend hours
mixing and matching, picking and choosing
the outfits she wears for school
but still doesn't know
how to write a resume
or how she should dress for an interview
how can she fight for independence
while still searching for
a man to pay the bill for her cell phone
and then lie down on her back
and give herself under the illusion
that being with any man is better than being alone
young man, how can you say
that she gave you her consent
because you took her "no" to mean "yes"
but on the same note young lady
how can you not see the image you project
when you call that strip of fabric you're wearing a dress?

how can you use the "N" word
when referring to your man
and not think it's derogatory
by changing that 'er' to an 'a'
you're carrying on today
the mindset of the men who hung
your ancestors from that tree
how can your soul mate be the man you hear
disrespecting you on the radio
how can you entertain the suggestion
that your part time profession be a scantily clad video ho
how can you flip through magazines
and marvel at the success
of hard-working millionaires
without taking a moment to contemplate the reality
that you, too, could end up there
how is it that you're willing
to spend, without a second thought,
$200 on a pair of pants or shoes
but, yet, when classes roll around
you're in the bookstore for hours
searching for that little yellow sticker that says, "used"
Black woman, how can you let her grow up
thinking all a mother should require from a man
is that he provide a roof and food on the table
why is she taught at a young age
the art of getting over

when she is physically and mentally able

why isn't she told

that abortion should never be considered

as a method for birth control

that, more than messing up your body

they tend to harden your heart

and oftentimes stain your soul

Black people, my poem is yearning

it's straining to sing

to everyone its song

it's trying to reach you

it's trying to teach you

that so many things have been going wrong

yet, it's never too late

to correct the mistakes

it's never too late

to produce love from hate

it's never too late to open up the gate

and show our young Black women

the art of living

we may not have the Partridge family

the Cleavers or the Bradys

but don't let that be an excuse

for not raising our young girls to be young ladies

we must guide them with love

never put them down

show them what it means to be cherished

make them believe

that in this world they will never be alone

and our dedication to them will never perish

my poem is shedding tears of realization for us all:

it takes a village to raise one little black girl

because united we stand, but divided- we fall

Promiscuity

Her soul bled

red

as her thighs spread

on the sheet less bed

thinking her hunger was fed

not knowing her brain was dead

until I spoke up and read

her story

I know she can hear me

my voice a stream of

constant quiet endless noise

as she stands prim and poised

on the stroll

on the track

she arches her back

and sticks out her tongue

thinking her physical maturation

makes up for her mind being young

her song is sung

life written out

story told from new to old

ever since she defined

Promiscuity

picking out of that the word

PROMIS

with no 'e' on the end

thinking surely, this time,
things could begin
all over again
she could be a
ho turned into a housewife
a whore with so much more
potential
that's what she thought when she was
laid up in that rental
legs splayed and
eyes sprayed with
misty visions of being paid
for her services
emitting low moans and
well-rehearsed groans
this Queen's only throne was in the
back seat of his jeep
or dark alley down the street
'cuz $39.99 at Motel 6
wasn't even as cheap
as she was
she hears that buzz
of my voice in her mind
every time she goes blind
from the reality that time
has forced upon her
she tells herself she knows

exactly what's the deal
she's only doing this until
she can finish paying bills
but she knows the real
disillusioned into thinking her
pimp can be her man
not allowing the truth to set in
and make her understand
that her ultimate plan was revealed
by the all too familiar click-clack of her heels
her mind reels as she attempts to
keep track of her tricks
I mean dates
as she slowly starts
loving to hate
then hating to love
her prism, her temple
while gazing above
at the ceiling
thoughts revealing
losing all hope of feeling
that PUSSY is anything more
than an acronym so true:
Publicly
Universally
Substantially
Servicing

<u>Y</u>*ou*

my words are reflective of

all that she'll do

yet I don't judge

I don't stare

but I don't pretend not to care

that every slap on her ass

and every pull of her hair

strips her bare

so I dare

I dare to hope that she can still feel

that her pride is worth more than a

5, 10, 20 dollar bill

she used to be agelessly wise

but now uses her ass to entice

and get closer to the guys

who only utilize her head

by pushing it down while they drive

she almost welcomes her demise

thinking it'll erase all the lies

she's built up inside

while I still whisper she's more than

just a pretty face

all thoughts of living instead of surviving

have begun to erase

and the PROMIS she once held onto

has begun to be based

on skimpy clothes and stilettos
worn by her fellow hoes
while she's breading her pimp
and taking care of her trick
she's becoming mind-whipped
by 1001 controlling dicks
constantly continuously finding inventing
new and creative ways to stick
in her conscience
see, now it's all beginning to make sense
she walked down that street called teasing
then turned around the corner called pleasing
but somehow got mixed up
at the sign marked believing
a good girl gone bad
a story too common to make us sad
as we sit back and remember
the encounters that we've had
with pretty, intelligent, seemingly
promising beauties
made to believe their purpose
will never be anything more
than to be posterchildren for
Promiscuity

Sometimes I Wonder

I'm not a poet, per se
I just relieve my mind
of the burdens placed upon it
by the unrelenting bullshit
I see going on everyday
there are all these thoughts
all these questions
all these emotions
running through my mind
pushing themselves out through the
drip of the ink from the pen
that took on a life of itself
when writing this poem
sometimes I wonder…
when the terms "my man" and "my woman"
became socially acceptable
I thought we fought for the right
to not be considered property
but, then again, all we remember from
Martin, Malcolm and Marcus is
I have a dream
By Any Means Necessary and
let's all go back to Africa
how are we supposed to go *back* somewhere
hardly any of us have ever been
and the only images we see in the media of those who

"represent" us are
young brothers on the streets
and 20 year old mothers of three
and crack babies and dope fiends and
modern day minstrel replicas of
us imitating them imitating us
sometimes I wonder...
when we stopped raising our fists
and promoting Black power
and started opening up our hands
to beg for a dollar
we are a race of culture, heritage and pride
but spend more time learning how to be
somebody's baby mamma than their bride
sometimes I wonder...
whatever happened to real Black music?
instead of 'My Girl' we have
'is that yo bitch?'
instead of sharing the wealth it's
nigga, I'm tryin' to get rich
claiming to be i.n.d.e.p.e.n.d.e.n.t
while asking your sugar daddy to
pay your rent
making millions reppin' silver change
with a name like 50 Cent
sometimes I wonder...
how you can buy that $20 bag of weed

but can't afford a 3 unit class

how you can complain about our kids

growing up too fast

but teach your 4 year old how to shake her ass

while her peers are finger-pain'ting

and getting ready for their naps

she's in her t-shirt and her panties

learning how to make it clap

sometimes I wonder…

why there are 900,000 Black men in prison

and 95% can't read above the 6th grade level

education by way of incarceration

has become nothing more than fabrication

a lesson from Penal Code 101

your time in the system will never be done

it's a trap, one we so willingly fall into

blaming the White man for our downfalls

instead of the one who looks like me and you

sometimes I wonder…

why people think lives will instantly change

just because we have a Black president

we have a history of not supporting each other

just look where our money is spent:

we spend over $500 billion as a people

each year

but the money only remains in our community for 4 hours

after that we go to Prada and Gucci and Polo

and front like our money gave us power
we got mad at Tommy Hilfiger
for saying his clothes aren't for us
Oprah said don't give him our money or time
they say ignorance is bliss
but it means lack of knowledge
because we were rockin Burberry
a rich, White clothing line
sometimes I wonder…
whoever decided poetry had to rhyme
if poetry is about releasing the words
pent up inside this vessel I call my mind
then how can I concern myself with
making sure
that the eighth syllable of the
last word of the
second sentence rhymes with the fourth?
I just want to stand here and
tell the world that the
shit flowing through me is nothing more
than an indicator of the society we live in
we love, we hate, we live, we die
we point fingers of blame
hoping somebody else takes responsibility
for all the things we want to change
we want more Black teachers
but we refuse to go to school

we want better health care for our people
but don't know the first doctor was Imhotep
we really believe weed makes us think clearer
but......damn
can't quite remember our last thought
we go to church every Sunday
but are self-proclaimed 6 day sinners
we think suicide is a cop-out
but tell me...
since when did knocks nodding on corners
count amongst the living?
we ridicule those who speak properly
accuse them of trying to be white
when pronouncing the ends of words
is simply trying to speak right
we let our mothers stay on section 8
our fathers gamble their lives away
our daughters raise themselves
our sons make more daughters
our sisters sell their bodies
our brothers sell their drugs
but we can't stand to hear a white man
call us a nigger
sometimes I wonder...
when we're gonna shed our
insecurities, our inabilities
our inhibitions, our indecisiveness

and embrace our collectiveness
until then I guess we'll remain content
with being whistled at
and getting disrespected
and responding when our men call out
"ay, come here, bitch'
our own music degrades us
history evades us
and the media portrays us an animalistic
so, sometimes I wonder…
when will "we" actually include
"you" and "me"
and, don't you see that not being locked up
doesn't make you free
and when will we be proud of our
big butts and big lips and
be thankful God gave Black women these
child-bearing hips
and when will we understand that
the American Dream has
red cheeks and blond hair
and as a Black woman
I'll never understand why some Black men
prefer to wander over there
while it may seem like I digress
let my words' impact hit you like thunder
it never ceases to amaze me all the things I sometimes wonder

Truth

Blacks are still in slavery
the only difference between the
slavery of the past and
slavery of the present
is we're presently enslaved
by choice
are you offended by my words?
ready to jump on the defensive track
and claim that my
thoughts are without merit
without validation
without truth
is your ignorance clouding your mind
allowing you to take a stand
against something you know
nothing about
if only you would take a moment to
break away from that
latest issue of Ebony, Essence or Jet
or remove your eyes from that
channel some call NET-
it's not for Blacks, it's become
Nigga Entertainment TV
or pry your ear away from the
bass lines and catchy tunes of
bullshit they now try to pass off as music

you would understand that
the knowledge you think you've obtained
has yet to be gained
and your so-called attempts to
enlighten your mind
have consistently been in vain
are you upset at my
questioning of your intelligence
embarrassed that I've
pulled your card beyond belief
is it my fault that you're a
mis-educated Negro
mis-led and mis-guided
by the misconceptions of the world
have you yet to realize that
the answers to all the questions
insecurities and unfairness
embedded in your mind are
at your fingertips
then again, finding those answers
would force you to do the unthinkable
the unimaginable
the unfathomable
you would have to read
don't roll your eyes and
turn your head at this
absurdity I'm presenting to you

and don't equate reading the
upcoming shows on the guide channel
or ingredients on the cereal box
or the public transportation schedules
with anything of substance
I'm talking about
reading where you've been
to know where you're at
to know where you're headed
we'll read the minute amount required
to get by in school
but we don't have to read
any more than that
we don't have to dig
any deeper than that
we don't have to search
for anything other than that
which we are force-fed
so we don't
we don't ponder the similarities
between the Bible and the Koran
and don't realize the words of the
religious guides many of us abide by
were written by an ordinary man
we complain about not being included
in the history books and the
lessons we're given throughout our schooling

but the reality is that we're choosing
not to read between the lines
although it's no question that
the society in which we reside
is full of technology and information
and in your face type of education
did I lose you
did you tune out when you realized
that the knowledge hitting your mind
is more powerful than me spitting a rhyme
could ever be
I'm not trying to preach to you
I'm merely trying to teach you
that you must be broken down
to be built back up
our minds need to be fed
just as our bodies do
only they require food for thought
nutrients we soak up from the
pages overflowing with knowledge
we insist that we're disadvantaged
the minority
always being held back by the
powers that be
have you yet to see that
a majority creates power, not numbers
if all our people came together

we could undoubtedly create wonders
but we're greedy, selfish
unwilling to help one another
to get to the top
we'll happily step on the necks
of our own sisters and brothers
we aspire to work for Microsoft
instead of buying if from Bill Gates
we support make-up companies
who lighten the skin tones
we are still raised to hate
we bypass the business section
of the newspaper in favor of the comics
and we still think Bamboozled was funny
how can you claim to be full of knowledge?
we think the Willie Lynch letter
was written by a man who was hung
and all we know about the Panthers
is they were Black and they were young
the only roots we're aware of
are those of Kizzy and Kunta
the only Spanish we bother to learn
are phrases like "Papi Cholo" or "punta"
you think this shit is funny
but the situation is frightening
everyday our level of ignorance
is steadily heightening

the Talented Tenth is not the
latest singing group
James Brown did not write
"Say it Loud, I'm Black and I'm Proud"
by his own volition
Aunt Jemima is more than just
a face on a bottle of syrup
Booker T. Washington was not
George Washington's brother
don't laugh
because you're the same one who claimed
the Cosby Show was unrealistic
because in your mind we're supposed to
remain intellectually confined
satirical
everyday performers wearing blackface
without the pain't
we have a history
of pride and unity
yet the word "I" is all too common
in many of our vocabularies
we despise stereotypes and
generalizations about our people
without admitting they originated
from somewhere
how can we claim contentment
with our present situations

and not come to the obvious
conclusion that our
crabs in a barrel mentality
has been self-created by those
resembling you and me
we complain about the glass ceiling
but don't use our raised fists
to break it
we cry about not getting the jobs
we know we're unqualified for
we pray to God for
strength, courage and wisdom
to deal with the problems we've created
and we still back it up
make it clap
and drop it like it's hot on cue
is this hitting home to you?
you have no knowledge of self
of your people
of your past, present or future
a lost individual in a pack
of lost souls who in turn
make up a lost race
everything we ever wanted to know
is right there in front of us
within reach
but we can't grasp it because

we've tied our own hands behind our backs

we've shackled our own ankles together

so we can't walk steer from our self made course

we've gagged ourselves so that

we can't speak on the truths

staring us in our faces

self-imposed captivity has become

our own form of slavery

our bodies are being held hostage

along with our minds

because we simply refuse to take the time

to become more than merely

educated fools

so let's stop with the excuses

take an hour away from tv shows

that are useless

there's no reason for ignorance in 2010

I will give you a book if it will make you begin

to open your eyes

and read

Glamour

I don't know the reason
for glamorizing the ghetto fabulous mentality
I see so many people who
have become rich in the art of
learning to be poor
poor in mind, body and spirit
they love to drown in sorrow's pit
but I've always been told that I'm "different"
could it be because I've never
snuck through the back doors on the bus
or demanded a line of credit at the corner store
or because I was brought up with the belief
that food stamps and welfare
were merely a means to an end
I didn't know that I was to sit back and
become content
with trading chunks of government cheese
on the days that wish sandwiches were only a dream
and spoiled milk substituted for sour cream
you must continuously remind me
for I often forget
I'm unaware of how it feels to
stand out on MacArthur and
turn tricks and trade licks and suck dicks
in hopes that it will lift me to a higher place
higher than her mother gets

from the many hits she takes at night on the pipes
her little sister kicks around outside
and her brother sells from the window of
his ride
should I apologize for thinking duck and cover
was only for earthquake drills in
elementary school?
I'll be damned but I've never had bullets fly past me
so I guess I'm not cool
does that mean I should say I'm sorry?
explain to you that
I was raised in the suburbs and didn't know
what was the meaning of E.S.O.
and I went to school with young, rich Whites
who drove BMW's instead of riding bikes
I've been asked how often I wash my hair
and is being ashy different from being scaly
and why do my skirts rise higher in the back than the front
but around those from your part of town
I'm white-washed and proper and don't know where I come from
since I never ate chitterlings or pigs feet
or even a slice of hog head cheese
and my name doesn't end in "iqua" or "asha"
and my hair isn't colored in 10 different shades
and I didn't have 3 little babies by
different no-good men
you say you can tell the ghetto is not where I was made

how ironic

would it be better if I told you

I come from a lineage of

despair and disgrace and in your face

ghetto mentalities

if I sobbed out stories telling you my

grandfather was imprisoned for murder and my father for

accessory to murder and my brother for murder

and my grandmother was shooting up

drugs she purchased

from her youngest son and

alcoholism was the addiction of choice and

3 way calling from jails and prisons was blocked and

in my family, powdered cocaine just didn't measure up to crack

rock and

homosexuals were homophobic while they feared exactly what they

craved and

substitute stand-ins disrespected the very thing

they preached for you to save

from a world where graduations were

few and far between and

those before me weren't brought up to believe

in the red, black and green and

single mothers defined the second shift

before that book was even a thought and

biological sperm donors stood in the shadows

ingesting the same poison

their customers bought
THAT'S where I come from
but maybe that isn't "ghetto" enough for you
isn't "real" enough for you
isn't enough to put me on "your level"
so once again, I guess I'm sorry
sorry for choosing not to be a product of many who've come before
because somebody out there wanted
me to be more
so I learned to say "isn't" instead of "ain't"
found myself saying
"ghost" rather than "hain't"
but still won't hesitate to
roll my eyes and my neck
while tellin' you my shit don't stank
because I'm versatile
could ride in a Bentley or the
back of the local bus with the same amount of dignity
could order a dollar menu sandwich with cheese-
and a filet mignon with the same amount of ease
I can stand here and boast of a degree
from one of the top public universities
and for that, I'll be damned if I apologize!
I won't say I'm sorry for not calling my man my nigga
my girls my bitches
for not thinking Moscato is a

high quality spirit
for not calling the act of intimacy
"beatin up my shit"
I will no longer apologize for taking pride
in not being just another ghetto girl from these ghetto streets
because I don't agree with
glamorizing the ghetto fabulous mentality

Just Me

In a world full of
hypocrisy, contradictions
falsities and surrealism
I humble myself
standing here before you
I find myself questioning myself
second guessing myself
having regrets for myself
and things get a little clearer
a little realer
and I am no longer unsure of my role
although you say I've been playing the role
been portraying the role
of someone other than myself
all in the midst of finding myself
while feeling lost at the same time
been walking around blind
to the reactions of my surroundings
been so stuck on fitting in
on wanting people to like me, to feel me
so you say I have lost sight of me
the real me
but I haven't
and I don't want you to
don't want you to label me, to categorize me
to judge me

but I already know you will

because this is the way our society works

we hear the things we want to hear

pay attention to the words that buffer the real

because it's easy

it's easy to choose ass over class

and since that's what you say

I presented to you

that's what you chose

and I'm real enough with myself to know

that I'm the only one to blame

so I stand here now

stripping myself bare without

taking any clothes off

because although you've already

jumped to your conclusions about

who I am and what I represent

I know that I am more than what you think

more than what you choose to talk about

in closed circles after

patting me on the back and shaking my hand

but I'm well aware that it's more feasible

more reasonable

for you to merely scratch the surface of me

and I don't expect you to dig any deeper

don't expect you to look any further

than what stands before you

so, to a certain extent, this is me
a strong Black woman
who embraces weakness far too often
a lover who fights with herself
more than you'll ever know
judgment by others and the criticism
of those who will never have the balls
to do what I do, what I've done
have nothing on internal conflict
so, unlike others, I place blame solely
on my shoulders
until this point I have not recognized
the power my words have over others
have not realized I can
hold a crowd captive
with my silence
can make you feel the intensity of my words
with only a glance
someone once told me I was
destined for greatness
and I forgot that
lost sight of that
turned a blind eye to that
all because I started writing for you instead of to you
got caught up in snaps and claps,
laughter and responses
but the message got lost in translation

so here it is:

I represent the many facets of a woman

sometimes smart, sometimes stupid

sometimes standing for something

sometimes falling for anything

sometimes uncomplicated

sometimes full of simple complexities

I am no better than the next woman

yet every day I'm striving to be

you may not like me

you may not feel me

you may not understand me

but you will listen to me

you will continue to pick and choose

which of my words you would like to use

against me

which of my poems you think are "real"

and which ones you have chosen as

whispered ladies room banter or

old ass locker room talk

but let me let you in on a little secret:

I have but one face looking back at me

in the mirror

but one person to answer to at the

end of my days

I hold myself accountable for my actions

and have never looked to you, or you, or you for validation

I speak on truths

whether it's putting your child before your man

or not making a living selling street pharmaceuticals

or questioning the media's portrayals of

our people

but as soon as I speak on sex

in a manner that makes you squirm

with excitement and discomfort

I'm wrong, I've changed, and I'm no longer "down for the cause"

if these are your thoughts

then fuck you

I have never claimed to be a conscious poet

never labeled myself as an artist who

only speaks on "safe topics"

never said that you should put me in a box

or high on a pedestal where I can remain

untouched

I am a spokesperson for those too scared of the possibilities of

your reactions

for people who are afraid to use their own voices to free

themselves

I'm trying to free myself with every stroke of my pen

and everything that I write comes from

deep within

whether I'm in jeans, a sweat suit or

a mini-skirt

I speak realities

I do my best to practice what I preach
I have learned from my mistakes
so I don't condemn things I'm guilty of
and I have yet to see you pay even
one of my bills
so your opinion of me becomes like an asshole-
something everyone has
and your judgment of me becomes
like a pimple on my nose
something I'll never need
so do me a favor:
listen to my words all the time
not just when a catchy phrase
sticks in your mind
stop remaining content with focusing
on one facet of me
when I've shown you so many repeatedly
but if you choose not to do this
I'll remain unaffected, unmoved, uncaring
because to know me is to respect me
fuck loving me, you can hate me
because if you do, I'll know I've evoked
an emotion in you greater than that
fake smile on your face reveals
and I can walk away from this mic
realizing that I have affected you
that you heard every word

that came out of my mouth
and whether you think it's all a lie
is up to you to decide
but rest assured, one way or another
you'll leave here tonight
with Brianni on your mind!

Price Tags

I'm racking my brain

trying to remember the last time I heard someone say

I have an item in my possession

so valuable, so special

that it should be placed on a pedestal

yet I want to give it away

when people put something on the curb

that looks unblemished

and place a 'free' sign in front of it

our immediate reaction is typically

'there must be something wrong with it'

simply because we aren't being asked to pay for it

which is ironic:

people look down on hoes

yet they're the only ones placing a value on it

and that's that bullshit

yet another example of judgment by those all too well-versed

in spouting it

nobody says shit about the ones reppin that

so called bff or convenient friend with benefits

I hear too many stories of women's self respect

being wrapped up in their reputations

in labels slapped on their backs

like nametags pressed to their chests

so they end up believing they CHOSE to be treated as less

once they decided to acknowledge their affinity for sex

that's the moment they became soiled
tainted
and they're only self proclaimed saving grace is
well at least I didn't make him pay for it
because it's okay to do what they do
as long as people don't catch wind of it
and that represents an even bigger problem amongst women
there is no sense of unity
instead of admitting many of us have been sluts
at one point or another
we'd rather get caught up on
'what does he think'
'what will she say'
'is there any way I can be honest without you looking at me like this'
instead, I'll look at her like this
because being better than at least one
is better than being labeled as just another one
of them
so keep hollerin' out that your pussy is priceless
and can't nobody put a monetary value on it
but don't forget you claim to be a dime
asking them to pay you in compliments
instead of crumbled up bills tossed carelessly on your dresser
because then you can still pretend that your name
is not synonymous with 'lesser'
I am she/am her/but not HER

ok being she/but don't confuse me with HER
am she only if her reflection is a good look on me
so take a good look at me
be mad at me
uncomfortable listening to me
cover eyes and close ears in hopes that I'll disappear
because anything is better than admitting you're no better
than a woman who will let her vagina don a price tag
just remember:
at the end of the day at least she can say
she owns her choices, no matter where she lays
while you're still low key
late night sneak fuckin' for free
taking walks of shame down yet another man's hallway

ABOUT THE AUTHOR

Brianni Blue is a woman of many talents, trials, and triumphs with a story to tell. Hailing from Berkeley, CA, Mrs. Blue is an Author, Orator, Poet, Spoken Word Artist, Host, Women's Rights Advocate, and Motivational Speaker.

Her unique, emotionally charged, tailored performances connect reality, entertainment, and inspiration to the goals, visions, and hopes of her audience.

Brianni has been invited to lend her creative, captivating brand of truth telling to events across the Unites States and on the national stage for TV One's broadcast performance show, "Verses and Flow." She has an online following of over 8,000, facilitates 'Wordsmith Wednesday,' a weekly writing segment on Facebook, and is the creator and host of Speak Easy- a widely popular weekly Open Mic Showcase in Oakland, CA.

Named the Best Female Spoken Word Artist in the 2014 Bay Area Black Music Awards and nominated for both a 2014 Oakland Indie Award and a 2014 H.O.P.E. Award, Brianni brings a fresh voice, presence, talent, and personality to engage an audience and give them the emotional push to take their success a step further.

Contact:
www.BriBlue.com
mrsbriblue@gmail.com
www.facebook.com/MrsBriBlue
www.twitter.com/MrsBriBlue
www.youtube.com/MrsBriBlue

Made in the USA
Monee, IL
28 April 2023